M000019788

DEVOTIONS
FOR
CONTENTMENT
&WISDOM

ECCLESIASTES & 1 CORINTHIANS

DEVOTIONS
FOR
CONTENTMENT
&WISDOM

ECCLESIASTES & 1 CORINTHIANS

Warren W. Wiersbe

HONOR HB BOOKS

Inspiration and Motivation for the Seasons of Life

COOK COMMUNICATIONS MINISTRIES
Colorado Springs, Colorado • Paris, Ontario
KINGSWAY COMMUNICATIONS LTD
Eastbourne, England

Honor Books® is an imprint of
Cook Communications Ministries, Colorado Springs, CO 80918
Cook Communications, Paris, Ontario
Kingsway Communications, Eastbourne, England

DEVOTIONS FOR CONTENTMENT AND WISDOM
© 2006 by Warren W. Wiersbe

All rights reserved. No part of this book may be reproduced without
written permission, except for brief quotations in books and critical
reviews. For information, write Cook Communications Ministries, 4050
Lee Vance View, Colorado Springs, CO 80918.

Cover Design: Jackson Design CO, LLC/Greg Jackson

First Printing, 2006
Printed in the United States of America

1 2 3 4 5 6 7 8 9 10 Printing/Year 10 09 08 07 06

Unless otherwise noted, Scripture quotations are taken from the HOLY
BIBLE, NEW INTERNATIONAL VERSION®. Copyright © 1973, 1978,
1984 by International Bible Society. Used by permission of Zondervan.
All rights reserved. Scripture quotations marked (KJV) are taken from the
King James Version of the Bible. (Public Domain); Scriptures marked
(TLB) are taken from *The Living Bible*, © 1971, Tyndale House Publishers,
Wheaton, IL 60189. Used by permission; and Scriptures marked "NKJV™"
are taken from the New King James Version®, Copyright © 1982 by
Thomas Nelson, Inc. Used by permission. All rights reserved. Italics in
Scripture have been added by the author for emphasis.

This book was originally published as two paperback editions in 1994
and 1995, compiled by Stan Campbell. Each devotional reading is
adapted from Warren Wiersbe's "Be" series.

Library of Congress Cataloging-in-Publication Data

Wiersbe, Warren W.
  Devotions for contentment and wisdom : Ecclesiastes-- 1 Corinthians / Warren
Wiersbe.
      p. cm. -- (60 days in the Word)
  Includes bibliographical references and index.
  ISBN 1-56292-700-0 (alk. paper)
  1. Bible. O.T. Ecclesiastes--Meditations. 2. Bible. N.T. Corinthians, 1st--
Meditations. I. Title.
  BS1475.54.W54 2006
  242'.2--dc22

                          2005026492

Contentment

Thirty Daily Readings from the Book of Ecclesiastes

People are never free of trying to be content." Ecologist Murray Bookchin wrote those words in the June 1, 1992, issue of the *London Independent*; more than a century earlier, the American naturalist Henry David Thoreau wrote, "The mass of men lead lives of quiet desperation."

Both men are right.

Today, we can go to the drugstore and buy mood elevators and even buy sleep enhancers, but we can't buy peace and contentment. If we want to escape the rat race, we can visit a theme park and purchase hours of entertainment; but the rat race will still be there when we walk out the gate. True contentment is a matter of the inner person: having the right priorities, measuring life by the right standards, focusing on the right goals, and exercising the right faith. It means taking God into every area of our life and letting Him have control.

If anybody knew the folly of living for the rat race (he called it "chasing after the wind"), it was King Solomon. He had everything, and he tried everything, and he recorded his experiments and experiences for us to read in an ancient book we call Ecclesiastes—"The Preacher."

The most recent self-help manual in the bookstore doesn't begin to give us the insights that Solomon shares in this journal of a man who tried to catch the wind. Solomon writes about success, leadership, life goals, social injustice, sex and marriage, money, and even old age and death. He honestly records his own feelings and failures and the lessons he learned from these experiments in the laboratory of life. He paid the price—we get all the benefits of his wisdom!

He tells us the master secret of having contentment in a world that wants to rob us of peace. Solomon points the way to the kind of lifestyle that makes living worthwhile and saves us from the dead-end streets of modern civilization.

Jesus said, "I have come that they may have life, and have it to the full" (John 10:10).

Solomon knew about that abundant life centuries ago, and you can know about it today. As each day you learn from King Solomon, you will discover that life can be satisfying and successful when you walk with God and trust Him.

Day 1

Solomon's Sequel

Read Ecclesiastes 1:1

The words of the Teacher, son of David, king in Jerusalem.
ECCLESIASTES 1:1

Nowhere in this book did the author give his name, but the descriptions he gave of himself and his experiences would indicate that the writer was King Solomon. Solomon began his reign as a humble servant of the Lord, seeking God's wisdom and help (1 Kings 3:5–15). As he grew older, his heart turned away from Jehovah to the false gods of the many wives he had taken from foreign lands (11:1ff). These marriages were motivated primarily by politics, not love, as Solomon sought alliances with the nations around Israel.

No amount of money or authority could stop the silent but sure ripening of divine judgment. The famous Scottish preacher Alexander Whyte said that "the secret worm … was gnawing all the time in the royal staff upon which Solomon leaned." The king's latter years were miserable because God removed His hand of blessing (1 Kings 11) and maintained Solomon's throne only because of His promise to his father, David (vv. 9–13; 2 Sam. 7:1–17).

Ecclesiastes appears to be the kind of book a person would write near the close of life, reflecting on life's experiences and the lessons learned. Solomon probably wrote Proverbs and the Song of Songs (Song of Solomon in the KJV) during the years he faithfully walked with God; and near the end of his life, he wrote Ecclesiastes. There is no record that King Solomon repented and turned to the Lord, but his message in Ecclesiastes suggests that he did.

Applying God's Truth:

1. What is the most foolish thing you've done out of love for someone?

2. If the wisest man who ever lived could not remain faithful to God, do you think it's realistic to expect that you can? Explain.

3. Based on Solomon's experiences, what would you say might be more important than wisdom in regard to continual spiritual growth?

Day 2

Whether Vain

Read Ecclesiastes 1:2

> *"Meaningless! Meaningless!" says the Teacher.*
> *"Utterly meaningless! Everything is meaningless."*
>
> ECCLESIASTES 1:2

Vanity of vanities," lamented Solomon, "all is vanity!" (according to the KJV of v. 2). Solomon liked that word "vanity"; he used it in some form thirty-eight times in Ecclesiastes as he wrote about everyday life. The word means emptiness, futility, vapor, that which vanishes quickly and leaves nothing behind.

From the human point of view ("under the sun," v. 3), life does appear futile, and it is easy for us to get pessimistic. The Jewish writer Sholom Aleichem once described life as "a blister on top of a tumor, and a boil on top of that." We can almost feel that definition!

The American poet Carl Sandburg compared life to "an onion— you peel it off one layer at a time, and sometimes you weep." And Irish-born British playwright George Bernard Shaw said that life is "a series of inspired follies."

What a relief to turn from these pessimistic views and hear Jesus Christ say, "I have come that they may have life, and have it to the full" (John 10:10). Or to read Paul's majestic declaration, "Therefore, my dear brothers, stand firm. Let nothing move you. Always give yourselves fully to the work of the Lord, because you know that your labor in the Lord is not in vain" (1 Cor. 15:58).

Life is not in vain if it is lived according to the will of God, and that is what Solomon teaches in this neglected and often misunderstood book.

Applying God's Truth:

1. Have you ever gone through periods when you considered your life and felt that all was vanity (meaningless)?

2. How would you define your current philosophy of life in a couple of sentences?

3. What relationships and activities provide the most meaning in your life?

Day 3

Problems Then and Now

Read Ecclesiastes 1:3

What does man gain from all his labor at which he toils under the sun?
ECCLESIASTES 1:3

What is the practical application of this book for us today? Is Ecclesiastes nothing but an interesting exhibit in a religious museum, or does it have a message for people in the space age?

Its message is for today. After all, the society that Solomon investigated a millennium before the birth of Christ was not too different from our world today. Solomon saw injustice to the poor, crooked politics, incompetent leaders, guilty people allowed to commit more crime, materialism, and a desire for the good old days. It sounds up-to-date, doesn't it?

If you have never trusted Jesus Christ as your Savior, then this book urges you to do so without delay. Why? Because no matter how much wealth, education, or social prestige you may have, life without God is futile. You are only "chasing after the wind" if you expect to find satisfaction and personal fulfillment in the things of the world. "What good is it for a man to gain the whole world, yet forfeit his soul?" asked Jesus in Mark 8:36.

Solomon experimented with life and discovered that there was no lasting satisfaction in possessions, pleasures, power, or prestige. He had everything, yet his life was empty! There is no need for you and me to repeat these experiments. Let's accept Solomon's conclusions and avoid the heartache and pain that must be endured when we experiment in the laboratory of life.

Applying God's Truth:

1. What have you witnessed or experienced lately that caused you to question the fairness of life?

2. What are some of the things you've tried in an attempt to bring more meaning to your life?

3. How would you contrast the quality of your life before a relationship with Jesus with your life afterward?

Day 4

As Sure as the World

Read Ecclesiastes 1:4–8

Generations come and generations go, but the earth remains forever.
ECCLESIASTES 1:4

From the human point of view, nothing seems more permanent and durable than the planet on which we live. When we say that something is as sure as the world, we are echoing Solomon's confidence in the permanence of Planet Earth. With all of its diversity, nature is uniform enough in its operation that we can discover its laws and put them to work for us. In fact, it is this dependability that is the basis for modem science.

Nature is permanent, but we are transient, mere pilgrims on earth. Our pilgrimage is a brief one, for death finally claims all of us. At the very beginning of his book, Solomon introduced a topic frequently mentioned in Ecclesiastes: the brevity of life and the certainty of death.

Individuals and families come and go, nations and empires rise and fall, but nothing changes, for the world remains the same. Thomas Carlyle called history a mighty drama, enacted upon the theater of time, with suns for lamps and eternity for a background. Solomon would add that the costumes and sets may occasionally change, but the actors and the script remain pretty much the same; and that is as sure as the world.

Applying God's Truth:

1. How frequently do you think about your inevitable death? How does it make you feel?

2. How do you try to ensure that you're making the most of your life while you have the opportunity?

3. As a member of your generation, how well are you connected to the older generation(s) as well as the younger one(s)?

Day 5

Everything Old Is New Again

Read Ecclesiastes 1:9–11

Is there anything of which one can say, "Look! This is something new"? It was here already, long ago; it was here before our time.

Ecclesiastes 1:10

A young man approached me at a conference and asked if he could share some new ideas for youth ministry. He was very enthusiastic as he outlined his program, but the longer I listened, the more familiar his ideas became. I encouraged him to put his ideas into practice but then told him that we had done all of those things in Youth for Christ before he was born and that YFC workers were still doing them. He was a bit stunned to discover that there was indeed "nothing new under the sun" (v. 9).

Solomon wrote, of course, about the basic principles of life and not about methods. As the familiar couplet puts it: "Methods are many, principles are few / methods always change, principles never do." The ancient thinkers knew this truth. The Stoic philosopher Marcus Aurelius wrote, "They that come after us will see nothing new, and they who went before us saw nothing more than we have seen." The only people who really think they have seen something new are those whose experience is limited or whose vision can't penetrate beneath the surface of things. Because something is recent, they think it is new; they mistake novelty for originality.

Applying God's Truth:

1. What are some of the principles you have held throughout your life that are identical to those of your parents and preceding generations?

2. How would you distinguish between novelty and originality?

3. If it's true that there is "nothing new under the sun," why do you think people today put so much emphasis on new and improved, new and better, and other promises of hitherto undiscovered products and services?

Day 6

Living in Circles

Read Ecclesiastes 1:12–18

I applied myself to the understanding of wisdom, and also of madness and folly, but I learned that this, too, is a chasing after the wind. For with much wisdom comes much sorrow; the more knowledge, the more grief.

ECCLESIASTES 1:17–18

When Adam and Eve sinned, they did get an experiential knowledge of good and evil, but since they were alienated from God, this knowledge only added to their sorrow. It has been that way with people ever since. Whether it is jet planes, insecticides, or television, each advance in human knowledge and achievement only creates a new set of problems for society.

For some people, life may be monotonous and meaningless; but it does not have to be. For Christians, life is an open door, not a closed circle; there are daily experiences of new blessings from the Lord. True, we can't explain everything; but life is not built on explanations: It is built on promises—and we have plenty of promises in God's Word!

The scientist tells us that the world is a closed system, and nothing is changed. The historian tells us that life is a closed book, and nothing is new. The philosopher tells us that life is a deep problem, and nothing is understood.

But Jesus Christ is "the power of God and the wisdom of God" (1 Cor. 1:24), and He has miraculously broken into history to bring new life to all who trust Him. If you are living in circles, then turn your life over to Him.

Applying God's Truth:

1. Do you think Solomon's observation that "the more knowledge, the more grief" is the same as declaring that ignorance is bliss? Why?

2. Do you agree that "with much wisdom comes much sorrow"? Give some specific examples to support your answer.

3. In what ways do you feel you may be living in circles?

Day 7

When Pleasure Is Treasured

Read Ecclesiastes 2:1–11

*I denied myself nothing my eyes desired; I refused my heart no pleasure.... Yet
when I surveyed all that my hands had done ... everything was meaningless.*

ECCLESIASTES 2:10–11

Today's world is pleasure mad. Millions of people will pay almost
any amount of money to buy experiences and temporarily escape
the burdens of life. While there is nothing wrong with innocent fun,
those who build their lives only on seeking pleasure are bound to be
disappointed in the end.

Why? For one thing, pleasure seeking usually becomes a selfish
endeavor, and selfishness destroys true joy. People who live for pleasure often exploit others to get what they want, and they end up with
broken relationships as well as empty hearts. People are more important than things and thrills. We are to be channels, not reservoirs; the
greatest joy comes when we share God's pleasure with others.

If people live for pleasure alone, enjoyment will decrease unless
the intensity of the pleasure increases. Then they reach a point of
diminishing returns when there is little or no enjoyment at all, only
bondage. For example, the more people drink, the less enjoyment
they get out of it. This means they must have more drinks and
stronger drinks in order to have the same pleasure; the sad result is
desire without satisfaction. Instead of alcohol, substitute drugs, gam-
bling, promiscuous sex, money, fame, or any other pursuit, and the

principle will hold true: When pleasure alone is the center of life, the result will ultimately be disappointment and emptiness.

Applying God's Truth:

1. On a scale of 1 (least) to 10 (most), to what extent would you say you are a pleasure seeker?

2. In what ways do people you know try to use pleasure to find fulfillment in life?

3. How can you enjoy life to the fullest, without having your pleasurable experiences diminish in effectiveness?

Day 8

Money Management

Read Ecclesiastes 2:12–23

> *I hated all the things I had toiled for under the sun, because I must*
> *leave them to the one who comes after me. And who knows*
> *whether he will be a wise man or a fool?*
>
> ECCLESIASTES 2:18–19

Solomon was born wealthy, and great wealth came to him because he was the king. But he was looking at life "under the sun" and speaking for the common people who were listening to his discussion. The day would come when Solomon would die and leave everything to his successor. This reminds us of our Lord's warning in the parable of the rich fool (Luke 12:13–21) and Paul's words in 1 Timothy 6:7–10. A Jewish proverb says, "There are no pockets in shrouds."

Money is a medium of exchange. Unless it is spent, it can do little or nothing for us. We can't eat money, but we can use it to buy food. It will not keep us warm, but it will purchase fuel for that purpose. A writer in the *Wall Street Journal* called money an article that may be used as a universal passport to everywhere except heaven and as a universal provider of everything except happiness.

Of course, you and I are stewards of our wealth; God is the Provider (Deut. 8:18) and the Owner, and we have the privilege of enjoying it and using it for His glory. One day we will have to give an account of what we have done with His generous gifts. While we cannot take wealth with us when we die, we can send it ahead as we use it today according to God's will (Matt. 6:19–34; 1 Tim. 6:17–19).

Applying God's Truth:

1. To what extent would you say you are concerned about leaving a good inheritance for your children? Do you wonder if they will appreciate it as they should?

2. What is your philosophy of money? How much importance do you think it deserves?

3. What does it mean to you to be a steward of your wealth?

Day 9

Eat, Drink, and Be Thankful

Read Ecclesiastes 2:24–26

*A man can do nothing better than to eat and drink and
find satisfaction in his work. This too, I see, is from the hand
of God, for without him, who can eat or find enjoyment?*

ECCLESIASTES 2:24–25

Solomon was not advocating "Eat, drink, and be merry, for tomorrow
we die!" That is the philosophy of fatalism, not faith. Rather, he was
saying, "Thank God for what you do have, and enjoy it to the glory of
God." Paul gave his approval to this attitude when he exhorted us to
trust in God, "who richly provides us with everything for our enjoyment" (1 Tim. 6:17).

Solomon made it clear that not only were the blessings from God,
but even the enjoyment of the blessings was God's gift to us (Eccl.
2:24). He considered it evil if a person had all the blessings of life
from God but could not enjoy them (6:1–5). It is easy to see why the
Jewish people read Ecclesiastes at the Feast of Tabernacles, for
Tabernacles is their great time of thanksgiving and rejoicing for God's
abundant provision of their needs. The farmer who prayed at the
table, "Thanks for good food and for good digestion," knew what
Solomon was writing about.

The important thing is that we seek to please the Lord (2:26) and
trust Him to meet our every need. God wants to give us wisdom,
knowledge, and joy; these three gifts enable us to appreciate His
blessings and take pleasure in them. It is not enough to possess things;

we must also possess the kind of character that enables us to use things wisely and enjoy them properly.

Applying God's Truth:

1. What are your Top Ten blessings from God?

2. For each of the things you have listed, are you experiencing the degree of enjoyment that you feel you should? If not, how can you enjoy them even more?

3. How can you develop the kind of character that enables you "to use things wisely and enjoy them properly"?

Day 10

Times and Seasons

Read Ecclesiastes 3:1–8

There is a time for everything, and a season for every activity
under heaven: a time to be born and a time to die.

ECCLESIASTES 3:1–2

We don't have to be a philosopher or a scientist to know that times and seasons are a regular part of life, no matter where we live. Were it not for the dependability of God-ordained natural laws, both science and daily life would be chaotic, if not impossible. Not only are there times and seasons in this world, but there is also an overruling providence in our lives. From before our birth to the moment of our death, God is accomplishing His divine purposes, even though we may not always understand what He is doing.

Solomon affirmed that God is at work in our individual lives, seeking to accomplish His will. All of these events come from God, and they are good in their time. The inference is plain: If we cooperate with God's timing, life will not be meaningless. Everything will be beautiful in its time (v. 11), even the most difficult experiences of life.

Things like abortion, birth control, mercy killing, and surrogate parenthood make it look as though humanity is in control of birth and death, but Solomon said otherwise. Birth and death are not human accidents; they are divine appointments, for God is in control. Psalm 139:13–16 and Ephesians 2:10 agree that God has so woven us in the womb that our genetic structure is perfect for the work He has prepared for us to do. We may foolishly hasten our death, but we cannot prevent it when our time comes, unless God so wills it.

Applying God's Truth:

1. Read Ecclesiastes 3:1–8 and identify any of the times and seasons you seem to be going through right now.

2. Can you think of an instance when recognizing God's timing brought meaning to your life? In what way?

3. How might you discover more meaning in life by letting go of certain things and turning to God instead?

Day 11

Enjoyment and Eternity

Read Ecclesiastes 3:9–22

> *I know that there is nothing better for men than to be happy*
> *and do good while they live. That everyone may eat and drink,*
> *and find satisfaction in all his toil—this is the gift of God.*
>
> ECCLESIASTES 3:12–13

When the well-known British Methodist preacher William Sangster learned that he had progressive muscular atrophy and could not get well, he made four resolutions and kept them to the end: (1) I will never complain; (2) I will keep the home bright; (3) I will count my blessings; (4) I will try to turn it to gain. This is the approach to life that Solomon wants us to take.

However, we must note that Solomon is not saying, "Don't worry—be happy!" He is promoting faith in God, not "faith in faith" or "pie in the sky, by and by." Faith is only as good as the object of faith, and the greatest object of faith is the Lord. He can be trusted.

How can life be meaningless and monotonous for us when God has made us a part of His eternal plan? We are not insignificant insects, crawling from one sad annihilation to another. Since we have trusted Jesus Christ, we are children of God being prepared for an eternal home. The Puritan pastor Thomas Watson said, "Eternity to the godly is a day that has no sunset; eternity to the wicked is a night that has no sunrise."

The proper attitude for us is fear of the Lord (v. 14 KJV), which is not the cringing of a slave before a cruel master, but the submission of an obedient child to a loving parent. If we fear God, we need not fear anything else, for He is in control.

Applying God's Truth:

1. What are four resolutions you could make to help you better cope with the difficult periods of life?

2. In what ways do you feel God is preparing you now for your eternal home?

3. How would you define "fear of the Lord" to someone hearing the phrase for the first time?

Day 12

Disorder in the Court

Read Ecclesiastes 4:1–6

I saw the tears of the oppressed—and they have no comforter; power was on the side of their oppressors—and they have no comforter. And I declared that the dead, who had already died, are happier than the living, who are still alive.

ECCLESIASTES 4:1–2

Solomon went into a courtroom to watch a trial, and there he saw innocent people being oppressed by power-hungry officials. The victims wept, but their tears did no good. Nobody stood with them to comfort or assist them. The oppressors had all the power, and the victims were helpless to protest or ask for redress.

Why didn't Solomon do something about this injustice? After all, he was the king. Alas, even the king couldn't do a great deal to solve the problem. For once Solomon started to interfere with his government and reorganize things, he would have only created new problems and revealed more corruption. This is not to suggest that we today should despair of cleaning out political corruption. As Christian citizens, we must pray for all in authority and do what we can to see that just laws are passed and fairly enforced (1 Tim. 2:1–3). But it is doubtful that a huge administrative body like the one in Israel could ever be free of corruption or that a crusader could have improved the situation.

Edward Gibbon, celebrated author of *The History of the Decline and Fall of the Roman Empire*, said that political corruption was "the most infallible symptom of constitutional liberty." Perhaps he was right; for where there is freedom to obey, there is also freedom to disobey. Some of Solomon's officials decided they were above the law, and the innocent suffered.

Applying God's Truth:

1. In what ways do you think our court system permits injustices?

2. How do you feel when you become the victim of an injustice by someone wealthier or more influential than you? What, if anything, do you do to try to right the scales of justice?

3. Do you regularly pray for people in authority—even if they misuse their authority to take advantage of you and others?

Day 13

Two Threads Are Better Than One

Read Ecclesiastes 4:7–16

Two are better than one, because they have a good return for their work.
ECCLESIASTES 4:9

Two are certainly better than one when it comes to working (v. 9), because two workers can get more done. Even when they divide the profits, they still get a better return for their efforts than if they work alone. Also, it is much easier to do difficult jobs together, because one can be an encouragement to the other.

Two are better when it comes to walking (v. 10). Roads and paths in Palestine were not paved or even leveled, and there were many hidden rocks in the fields. It was not uncommon for even the most experienced traveler to stumble and fall, perhaps break a bone, or even tumble into a hidden pit (Ex. 21:33–34). How wonderful to have a friend who could help them up (or out).

Two are better than one when it comes to warmth (Eccl. 4:11). Two travelers camping out, or even staying in the courtyard of a public inn, would feel the cold of the Palestinian night and need one another's warmth for comfort. The only way to be warm alone was to carry extra blankets and add to their load.

Finally, two are better than one when it comes to their security, especially at night (v. 12). It was dangerous for anyone to travel alone, day or night; most people traveled in groups for fellowship and for safety.

If two travelers are better than one, then three would fare even

better. Solomon had more than numbers in mind; he was also thinking of the unity involved in three cords woven together (v. 12)—what
a beautiful picture of friendship!

Applying God's Truth:

1. What have you done lately to help someone's work go a little
easier?

2. What have you done lately to assist someone who has stumbled
in his or her spiritual walk and could use some help?

3. What kind of help could you use at this point in your life? Who
might be able to help if you alerted that person to your need?

Day 14

The Sacrifice of Fools

Read Ecclesiastes 5:1–7

Guard your steps when you go to the house of God. Go near to listen rather than to offer the sacrifice of fools, who do not know that they do wrong.

ECCLESIASTES 5:1

Solomon had visited the courtroom, the marketplace, the highway, and the palace. Now he paid a visit to the temple, that magnificent building whose construction he had supervised. He watched the worshippers coming and going, praising God, praying, sacrificing, and making vows. He noted that many of them were not at all sincere in their worship and that they left the sacred precincts in worse spiritual condition than when they had entered. What was their sin? They were robbing God of the reverence and honor He deserved. Their acts of worship were perfunctory, insincere, and hypocritical.

Even though God's glorious presence doesn't dwell in our church buildings as it did in the temple, believers today still need to heed this warning. The worship of God is the highest ministry of the church and must come from devoted hearts and yielded wills. For God's people to participate in public worship while harboring unconfessed sin is to ask for God's rebuke and judgment.

The important thing is that worshippers go near to listen, that is, to obey the Word of God. Sacrifices are not substitutes for obedience. Offerings in the hands without obedient faith in the heart become the sacrifice of fools, because only fools think they can deceive God. Fools think they are doing good, but they are only doing evil. And God knows it.

Applying God's Truth:

1. What kinds of sacrifices do people offer today that may be a substitute for genuine obedience to God?

2. What other forms of insincere worship take place in the church today?

3. How can you ensure that your own worship remains pure and sincere?

Day 15

Matters of Wealth and Health

Read Ecclesiastes 5:8–20

> *Whoever loves money never has money enough; whoever*
> *loves wealth is never satisfied with his income.*
>
> ECCLESIASTES 5:10

There is no escaping the fact that we need a certain amount of money in order to live in this world, but money itself is not the magic cure-all for every problem. John Wesley, cofounder of the Methodist church, told his people, "Make all you can, save all you can, give all you can." Wesley himself could have been a very wealthy man, but he chose to live simply and give generously.

The late Joe Louis, world heavyweight boxing champion, used to say, "I don't like money, actually, but it quiets my nerves." But Solomon said that possessing wealth is no guarantee that our nerves will be calm and our sleep sound. According to him, the common laborer sleeps better than the rich man (v. 12). *The Living Bible* expresses verse 12 perfectly: "The man who works hard sleeps well whether he eats little or much, but the rich must worry and suffer insomnia."

More than one preacher has mentioned John D. Rockefeller in his sermons as an example of a man whose life was almost ruined by wealth. At the age of fifty-three, Rockefeller was the world's only billionaire, earning about a million dollars a week. But he was a sick man who lived on crackers and milk and could not sleep because of worry. When he started giving his money away, his health changed radically, and he lived to celebrate his ninety-eighth birthday!

Yes, it is good to have the things that money can buy, provided we don't lose the things money can't buy.

Applying God's Truth:

1. Do you think there is a direct correlation between having an abundance of money and an abundance of peace? Why?

2. What do you think of Wesley's command to "make all you can, save all you can, give all you can"?

3. To what extent do you think that worrying about money is a source of other problems in your life? In what ways?

Day 16

Living Versus Existing

Read Ecclesiastes 6:1–9

> *All man's efforts are for his mouth, yet his appetite is never satisfied.*
> ECCLESIASTES 6:7

Rich and poor alike labor to stay alive. They must either produce food or earn money to buy it. The rich can let their money work for them, but the poor have to use their muscles if they and their families are going to eat. But even after all this labor, the appetite of neither rich nor poor is fully satisfied.

Why do we eat? So that we can add years to our life. But what good is it for us to add years to our life if we don't add life to our years? We are like the birds that I watch in the backyard. They spend all their waking hours either looking for food or escaping from enemies. (We have cats in our neighborhood.) These birds are not really living; they are only existing. Yet they are fulfilling the purposes for which the Creator made them—and they even sing about it!

Solomon is not suggesting that it is wrong either to work or to eat. Many of us enjoy doing both. But if our life consists only in working and eating, then we are being controlled by our appetites, and that almost puts us on the same level as animals. As far as nature is concerned, self-preservation may be the first law of life, but we who are made in the image of God must live for something higher.

Applying God's Truth:

1. Is your work a fulfilling activity for you? How could it become more fulfilling?

2. How much enjoyment do you get out of eating? Do you make the most out of your meals?

3. What things can you do to keep from letting routine activities (like working and eating) take control and prevent you from enjoying what is truly important in life?

Day 17

It's Your Choice

Read Ecclesiastes 6:10

> *Better what the eye sees than the roving of the appetite.... Whatever exists*
> *has already been named, and what man is has been known.*
> ECCLESIASTES 6:9–10

Since what's going to be is going to be, why bother to make decisions? Isn't it all predestined anyway? "Whatever exists has already been named, and what man is has been known" (v. 10). To the Jewish mind, giving a name to something is the same as fixing its character and stating what the thing really is. During the time of creation, God named the things He made; and nobody changed those designations. Light is light and not darkness; day is day and not night (Gen. 1:3–31).

Our name is "man"—Adam, meaning "from the earth" (Gen. 2:7). Nobody can change the fact that we came from the earth, and we will return to the earth (3:19). Man by any other name would still be man, made from the dust and eventually returning to the dust.

The fact that God has named everything does not mean that our world is a prison and that we have no freedom to act. Certainly God can accomplish His divine purposes with or without our cooperation, but He invites us to work with Him. We cooperate with God as we accept the names He has given to things: Sin is sin; obedience is obedience; truth is truth. If we alter these names, we move into a world of illusion and lose touch with reality. This is where many people are living today.

We are free to decide and choose our world, but we are not free to change the consequences. If we choose a world of illusion, we start living on substitutes, and there can be no satisfaction in a world of substitutes.

Applying God's Truth:

1. Does the fact that you serve an omniscient God make you feel that your life has less spontaneity and choice than it should have? Why?

2. What are some of the changes you would like to make in your life?

3. How do you think you might begin to cooperate with God to bring about some of the changes you have listed?

Day 18

Questioning God

Read Ecclesiastes 6:10–12

> *No man can contend with one who is stronger than he.*
> ECCLESIASTES 6:10

Solomon seems to say, "It just doesn't pay to argue with God or to fight God. This is the way life is, so just accept it and let God have His way. You can't win, and even if you do think you win, you ultimately lose."

But his is a negative view of the will of God. It gives the impression that God's will is a difficult and painful thing that should be avoided at all cost. Jesus said that God's will was the food that nourished and satisfied Him (John 4:32–34). It was meat, not medicine. The will of God comes from the heart of God and is an expression of the love of God (Ps. 33:11). What God wills for us is best for us because He knows far more about us than we do.

Why would we want to have our own way just for the privilege of exercising freedom? Insisting on having our own way isn't freedom at all; it is the worst kind of bondage. In fact, the most terrible judgment we could experience in this life would be to have God give us up and let us have our own way (Rom. 1:24, 26, 28).

God is free to act as He sees best. He is not a prisoner of His attributes, His creation, or His eternal purposes. You and I may not understand how God exercises His freedom, but it isn't necessary for us to know all. Our greatest freedom comes when we are lovingly lost in the will of God. Our Father in heaven doesn't feel threatened when we question Him, debate with Him, or even wrestle with Him, so long as we love His will and want to please Him.

Applying God's Truth:

1. What kind of emotions does the thought of God's will bring to your heart?

2. Do you think God is displeased when you question His will for you? Why?

3. Is it easy for you to trust that God knows best and leave things in His hands? Or do you want to understand everything that is going on as it is happening?

Day 19

Looking Death in the Face

Read Ecclesiastes 7:1–8

A good name is better than fine perfume,
and the day of death better than the day of birth.

ECCLESIASTES 7:1

Solomon was not contrasting birth and death, nor was he suggesting that it is better to die than to be born because people can't die unless they have been born. He was contrasting two significant days in human experience: the day a person is given a name and the day when that name shows up in the obituary column. The life lived between those two events will determine whether that name leaves behind a lovely fragrance or a foul stench.

Solomon is advising us to look death in the face and learn from it. He is not saying that we should be preoccupied with death, because that could be abnormal. But there is a danger that we may try to avoid confrontations with the reality of death and, as a result, not take life as seriously as we should. "Teach us to number our days aright, that we may gain a heart of wisdom" (Ps. 90:12).

The late Dr. Ernest Becker wrote in his Pulitzer Prize–winning book *The Denial of Death*: "The idea of death, the fear of it, haunts the human animal like nothing else; it is a mainspring of human activity—activity designed largely to avoid the fatality of death, to overcome it by denying in some way that it is the final destiny for man" (Free Press, 1975, p. ix). King Solomon knew this truth centuries ago!

Applying God's Truth:

1. In what ways does thinking about death help you take life more seriously?

2. Would you say you spend more time thinking back about the things you have done since you were born or thinking about what you hope to do before you die? Are you satisfied that your balance of the two is what it should be?

3. Would you say you are haunted by the fear of death, or is your eventual death something that inspires you to a greater faith in God? Explain.

Day 20

Seize the Day

Read Ecclesiastes 7:9–12

> *Do not say, "Why were the old days better than these?"*
> *For it is not wise to ask such questions.*
> ECCLESIASTES 7:10

An Arab proverb says, "Watch your beginnings." Good beginnings will usually mean good endings. The Prodigal Son started with happiness and wealth but ended with suffering and poverty (Luke 15:11–16). Joseph began as a slave but ended as a sovereign (Gen. 37—41)! God always saves the best wine until the last (John 2:10), but Satan starts with his best and then leads the sinner into suffering and perhaps even death.

When life is difficult and we are impatient for change, it is easy to long for the good old days when things were better. When the foundation was laid for the second temple, the old men wept for the good old days of the former temple, and the young men sang because the work had begun (Ezra 3:12–13). It has been said that the good old days are the combination of a bad memory and a good imagination, and often this is true.

Yesterday is past and cannot be changed, and tomorrow may not come; so we must make the most of today. *"Carpe diem!"* wrote the Roman poet Horace. "Seize the day!" This does not mean that we should not learn from the past or prepare for the future, because both are important. It means that we must live today in the will of God and not be paralyzed by yesterday or hypnotized by tomorrow. The

Victorian essayist Hilaire Belloc wrote, "While you are dreaming of the future or regretting the past, the present, which is all you have, slips from you and is gone."

Applying God's Truth:

1. In what ways do you try to "watch your beginnings"? Do you keep God's will in mind as you make plans?

2. When times are difficult, what are some things you can do to maintain a focus on the future rather than drifting into a longing for the past?

3. What can you do right now to "seize" today?

Day 21

The Best of Times, the Worst of Times

Read Ecclesiastes 7:13–29

> *When times are good, be happy; but when times are bad, consider:*
> *God has made the one as well as the other. Therefore, a man*
> *cannot discover anything about his future.*

ECCLESIASTES 7:14

Wisdom gives us perspective so that we aren't discouraged when times are difficult or arrogant when things are going well. It takes a good deal of spirituality to be able to accept prosperity as well as adversity, for often prosperity does greater damage.

God balances our lives by giving us enough blessings to keep us happy and enough burdens to keep us humble. If all we had were blessings in our hands, we would fall right over, so the Lord balances the blessing in our hands with burdens on our backs. That helps to keep us steady, and as we yield to Him, He can even turn the burdens into blessings.

Why does God constitute our lives in this way? The answer is simple: to keep us from thinking that we know it all and that we can manage our lives by ourselves. "A man cannot discover anything about his future" (v. 14). Just about the time we think we have an explanation for things, God changes the situation, and we have to throw out our formula. This is where Job's friends went wrong: They tried to use an old road map to guide Job on a brand-new journey, and the map didn't fit (Job 2:11—37:24). No matter how much experience we have in the Christian life, or how many books we read, we must still walk by faith.

Applying God's Truth:

1. Can you think of a recent time when you became discouraged during difficult circumstances? Or when you were arrogant when things were going well?

2. Do you feel you have a level of wisdom adequate enough to allow you to accept both adversity and prosperity? If not, what do you think you need to do?

3. During times of adversity do you try to see what God may be trying to teach you? Or are you usually too busy complaining?

Day 22

It Just Isn't Fair

Read Ecclesiastes 8:1–13

Although a wicked man commits a hundred crimes and still lives a long time, I know that it will go better with God-fearing men, who are reverent before God.

ECCLESIASTES 8:12

If there is no God, then we have nobody to blame but ourselves (or nothing but fate) for what happens in the world. But if we believe in a good and loving God, we must face the difficult question of why there is so much suffering in the world. Does God know about it and yet not care? Or does He know and care but lack the power to do anything about it?

Some people ponder this question and end up becoming either agnostics or atheists, but in so doing, they create a whole new problem: Where does all the good come from in the world? It is difficult to believe that matter alone produced the beautiful and enjoyable things we have in our world, even in the midst of so much evil.

Other people solve the problem by saying that evil is only an illusion and that we shouldn't worry about it or that God is in the process of evolving and can't do much about the tragedies of life. They assure us that God will get stronger and that things will improve as the process of evolution goes on.

Solomon didn't deny the existence of God or the reality of evil, nor did he limit the power of God. Solomon solved the problem of evil by affirming these factors and seeing them in their proper perspective.

During the darkest days of World War II, somebody asked a

friend of mine, "Why doesn't God stop the war?" My friend wisely replied, "Because He didn't start it in the first place." Solomon would have agreed with that answer.

Applying God's Truth:

1. When people ask your opinion, how do you explain the existence of suffering?

2. Do you think either God's power or His love is limited in any way? Explain.

3. Are you suffering in some way in which you need to apply what you believe?

Day 23

The First Step Toward Knowledge

Read Ecclesiastes 8:14–17

No one can comprehend what goes on under the sun. Despite all his efforts to search it out, man cannot discover its meaning.

ECCLESIASTES 8:17

People who have to know everything, or who think they know everything, are destined for disappointment in this world. Through many difficult days and sleepless nights, the Preacher applied himself diligently to the mysteries of life. He came to the conclusion that "no one can comprehend what goes on under the sun" (v. 17). Perhaps we can solve a puzzle here and there, but none of us can comprehend the totality of things or explain all that God is doing.

Historian Will Durant surveyed human history in his multivolume *Story of Civilization* and came to the conclusion that "our knowledge is a receding mirage in an expanding desert of ignorance." Of course, this fact must not be used as an excuse for stupidity. "The secret things belong to the LORD our God, but the things revealed belong to us and to our children forever, that we may follow all the words of this law" (Deut. 29:29). God doesn't expect us to know the unknowable, but He does expect us to learn all that we can and obey what He teaches us. In fact, the more we obey, the more He will teach us (John 7:17).

A confession of ignorance is the first step toward true knowledge. "The man who thinks he knows something does not yet know as he ought to know" (1 Cor. 8:2). The person who wants to learn God's truth must possess honesty and humility.

Applying God's Truth:

1. What are some of the mysteries of life that you frequently ponder?

2. How is your faith affected when you struggle with something you can't figure out?

3. Do you think there are things God doesn't want us to know, or should we keep struggling to understand the mysteries of life?

Day 24

A Final Appointment

Read Ecclesiastes 9:1–4

> *Anyone who is among the living has hope—even a*
> *live dog is better off than a dead lion!*
>
> ECCLESIASTES 9:4

I am not afraid to die," quipped Woody Allen. "I just don't want to be there when it happens." But he will be there when it happens, as must every human being, because there is no escaping death when our time has come. Death is not an accident—it is an appointment (Heb. 9:27 KJV), a destiny that nobody but God can cancel or change.

Life and death are in the hand of God (Eccl. 9:1), and only He knows our future, whether it will bring blessing (love) or sorrow (hatred). Solomon was not suggesting that we are passive actors in a cosmic drama, following an unchangeable script handed to us by an uncaring director. Throughout this book, Solomon has emphasized our freedom of discernment and decision. But only God knows what the future holds for us and what will happen tomorrow because of the decisions we make today.

"As it is with the good man, so with the sinner" (v. 2). "If so, why bother to live a godly life?" we may ask. "After all, whether we obey the law or disobey, bring sacrifices or neglect them, make or break promises, we will die just the same." Yes, we share a common destiny on earth—death and the grave—*but we do not share a common destiny in eternity*. For that reason, everybody must honestly face "the last enemy" (1 Cor. 15:26) and decide how to deal with it. How we deal with the reality of death reveals itself in the way we deal with the realities of life.

Applying God's Truth:

1. Have you placed your life in the hand of God? How about your death?

2. Is there anything you feel you need to do before you die? If so, are you working toward getting it done?

3. Does thinking about death inspire you to greater action or frighten you into passivity?

Day 25

When Hope Becomes Hopeless

Read Ecclesiastes 9:5–10

*The living know that they will die, but the dead know nothing; they have
no further reward, and even the memory of them is forgotten.*

ECCLESIASTES 9:5

What Solomon wrote about the dead can be reversed and applied to the living. The dead do not know what is happening on earth, but the living know and can respond to it. The dead cannot add anything to their reward or their reputation, but the living can. The dead cannot relate to people on earth by loving, hating, or envying, but the living can. Solomon was emphasizing the importance of seizing opportunities while we live, rather than blindly hoping for something better in the future, because death will end our opportunities on this earth.

"The human body experiences a powerful gravitational pull in the direction of hope," wrote journalist Norman Cousins, who survived a near-fatal illness and a massive heart attack before his death in 1990. "That is why the patient's hopes are the physician's secret weapon. They are the hidden ingredients in any prescription."

We endure because we hope, but "hope in hope" (like "faith in faith") is too often only a kind of self-hypnosis that keeps us from facing life honestly. While patients may be better off with an optimistic attitude, it is dangerous for them to follow a false hope that may keep them from preparing for death. That kind of hope is hopeless. When the end comes, the patients' outlook may be cheerful, but the outcome will be tragic.

Applying God's Truth:

1. If you knew you were to die soon, would your plans for today change in any way? How?

2. What are some opportunities you need to seize while you still have the time?

3. What is your definition of hope? Does your hope keep your faith strong?

Day 26

No Guarantees

Read Ecclesiastes 9:11–18

> *The race is not to the swift or the battle to the strong, nor does food*
> *come to the wise or wealth to the brilliant or favor to the learned;*
> *but time and chance happen to them all.*
>
> ECCLESIASTES 9:11

Anticipating the response of his listeners (and his readers), Solomon turned from his discussion of death and began to discuss life. If death is unavoidable, some would argue, then the smartest thing we can do is major on our strengths and concentrate on life. When death comes, at least we will have the satisfaction of knowing we worked hard and achieved some success.

"Don't be too sure of that!" Solomon would reply. "You can't guarantee what will happen in life, because life is unpredictable."

Our abilities are no guarantee of success (vv. 11–12). While it is generally true that the fastest runners win the races, the strongest soldiers win the battles, and the smartest and most skillful workers win the best jobs, it is also true that these same gifted people can fail miserably because of factors out of their control. Successful people know how to make the most of time and procedure (8:5), but only the Lord can control time and chance (9:11).

Of course, Christians don't depend on such things as luck or chance because their confidence is in the loving providence of God. Dedicated Christians don't carry a rabbit's foot or trust in lucky days or numbers. Canadian humorist Stephen Leacock said, "I'm a great believer in luck. I find that the harder I work, the more I have of it."

Christians trust God to guide them and help them in making decisions, and they believe that His will is best. They leave time and chance in His capable hands.

Applying God's Truth:

1. What would you say are your most significant strengths? In what ways do you try to count on those strengths for success?

2. Do you have any personal superstitions? To what extent do you tend to rely on luck or chance?

3. From this point on, how can you better leave time and chance completely in God's hands?

Day 27

Foolish Rulers

Read Ecclesiastes 10:1–10

Fools are put in many high positions, while the rich occupy the low ones.
I have seen slaves on horseback, while princes go on foot like slaves.

ECCLESIASTES 10:6–7

If there is one person who needs wisdom, it is the ruler of a nation. When God asked Solomon what gift he especially wanted, the king asked for wisdom (1 Kings 3:3–28). Lyndon B. Johnson said, "A president's hardest task is not to do what's right, but to know what's right." That requires wisdom.

If a ruler is proud, he may say and do foolish things that cause him to lose the respect of his associates (Eccl. 10:4). The picture here is of a proud ruler who easily becomes angry and takes out his anger on the attendants around him. Of course, if a man has no control over himself, how can he hope to have control over his people?

To be sure, there is a righteous anger that sometimes needs to be displayed (Eph. 4:26), but not everything we call righteous indignation is really righteous. It is so easy to give vent to jealousy and malice by disguising them as holy zeal for God. Not every religious crusader is motivated by love for God or obedience to the Word. Such zeal could be a mask that is covering hidden anger or jealousy.

But if a ruler is too pliable, he is also a fool (Eccl. 10:5–7). If he lacks character and courage, he will put fools in the high offices and qualified people in the low offices. The servants will ride on horses, while the noblemen will walk. If a ruler has incompetent people advising him, he is almost certain to govern the nation unwisely.

The best rulers (and leaders) are men and women who are tough minded but tenderhearted, who put the best people on the horses and don't apologize for it.

Applying God's Truth:

1. What bosses have you most respected? Which have you least respected? What caused the differences in your opinions?

2. Do you feel that you have sufficient control over yourself so that you can help control others? If not, what areas do you need to work on?

3. Would you say you are too proud? Too pliable? Or do you feel you are achieving an appropriate balance?

Day 28

Looking Out for Number One

Read Ecclesiastes 10:11–20

*Do not revile the king even in your thoughts, or curse the rich in
your bedroom, because a bird of the air may carry your words,
and a bird on the wing may report what you say.*

ECCLESIASTES 10:20

In recent years, various developing nations have seen how easy it is
for unscrupulous leaders to steal government funds in order to build
their own kingdoms. Unfortunately, it has also happened recently to
some religious organizations. The courts may not catch up with all the
unscrupulous politicians or ministers, but God will eventually judge
them, and His judgment will be just.

The familiar saying "A little bird told me" probably originated
from verse 20. It is easy to imagine the group of these officers having
a party in one of their private rooms, and instead of toasting the king,
they are cursing (making light of) him. Of course, they wouldn't do so
if any of the king's friends were present, but they are sure that the
company will faithfully keep the secret. Alas, somebody tells the king
what was said, and this gives him reason to punish the offenders or
dismiss them from their offices.

Even if we can't respect the person in the office, we must
respect the office (Rom. 13:1–7; 1 Peter 2:13–17). "You shall not
revile God, nor curse a ruler of your people" (Ex. 22:28 NKJV). These
hirelings were certainly indiscreet when they cursed the king, for
they should have known that one of their number would use this
event either to intimidate his friends or to ingratiate himself with

the ruler. A statesman asks, "What is best for my country?" A politician asks, "What is best for my party?" But a mere officeholder, a hireling, asks, "What is most profitable for me?"

Applying God's Truth:

1. Do you know of any ministries or religious organizations that have been shaken by scandals concerning their leaders? What was the root of the problem? What were the results?

2. Can you think of anything you have said today that might embarrass you if a little bird passed it along to someone else?

3. Think of a leader you don't particularly respect. What can you do to at least respect the office, if not the person?

Day 29

A Quest for Adventure

Read Ecclesiastes 11

Cast your bread upon the waters, for after many days you will find it again.
ECCLESIASTES 11:1

When I was a boy, I practically lived in the public library during the summer months. I loved books, the building was cool, and the librarians gave me the run of the place since I was one of their best customers. One summer I read nothing but true adventure stories written by real heroes like Frank Buck and Martin Johnson. These men knew the African jungles better than I knew my hometown! I was fascinated by *I Married Adventure*, the autobiography of Martin Johnson's wife, Osa. When Clyde Beatty brought his circus to town, I was in the front row watching him tame the lions.

Since those boyhood days, life has become a lot calmer for me, but I trust I haven't lost that sense of adventure. In fact, as I get older, I am asking God to keep me from getting set in my ways in a life that is routine, boring, and predictable. "I don't want my life to end in a swamp," said British expositor F. B. Meyer. I agree with him. When I trusted Jesus Christ as my Savior, I "married adventure"; and that meant living by faith and expecting the unexpected.

Solomon used two activities to illustrate his point: the merchant sending out his ships (vv. 1–2) and the farmer sowing his seed (vv. 3–6). In both activities, a great deal of faith is required because neither the merchant nor the farmer can control the circumstances. If the merchant and the farmer wait until the circumstances are ideal, they will never get anything done! Life has a certain amount of risk to it, and that's where faith comes in.

Applying God's Truth:

1. What was the last adventurous thing you did?

2. If you had a bit more faith in God, what new adventure would you like to try?

3. What is your usual attitude toward risk? Are you satisfied with it, or would you like to become more (or less) of a risk taker? How could you make any desired changes?

Day 30

Satisfaction Guaranteed

Read Ecclesiastes 12

*Fear God and keep his commandments, for this is the whole
duty of man. For God will bring every deed into judgment,
including every hidden thing, whether it is good or evil.*

ECCLESIASTES 12:13–14

People may seem to get away with sin (8:11), but their sins will eventually be exposed and judged righteously (vv. 12–13). Those who have not trusted the Lord Jesus Christ will be doomed forever. "The eternity of punishment is a thought which crushes the heart," said Charles Haddon Spurgeon. "The Lord God is slow to anger, but when He is once aroused to it, as He will be against those who finally reject His Son, He will put forth all His omnipotence to crush His enemies."

Six times in his discourse, Solomon told us to enjoy life while we can, but at no time did he advise us to enjoy sin. The joys of the present depend on the security of the future. If you know Jesus Christ as your Savior, then your sins have already been judged on the cross; and there is now no condemnation for those who are in Christ Jesus (Rom. 8:1; John 5:24). But if you die having never trusted Christ, you will face judgment at His throne and be lost forever (Rev. 20:11–15).

Is life worth living? Yes, if you are truly alive through faith in Jesus Christ. Then you can be satisfied, no matter what God may permit to come to your life.

"He who has the Son has life; he who does not have the Son of God does not have life" (1 John 5:12).

You can receive life in Christ and be satisfied.

Applying God's Truth:

1. Do you know any people who truly seem to think they will get by with their sinful actions? What can you learn from these persons?

2. Do you feel more satisfied with life now than you did when you began these readings? In what ways? What areas of life do you still need to work on?

3. What are three things you can do from now on that are likely to bring you a greater degree of satisfaction with life?

Wisdom

Thirty Daily Readings from the Book of 1 Corinthians

We live in the midst of a knowledge explosion so incredible that even the experts can't keep up with all the developments in their fields. More and more, people are having to specialize, and the specialists have to depend on each other.

Knowledge abounds, but wisdom languishes. Wisdom is the right use of knowledge. Knowledge has to do with *facts*, but wisdom thrives on *truths*. Knowledge prepares us to make a living, but wisdom enables us to make a life. Our world is rich in knowledge and poor in wisdom, and, tragically enough, the world doesn't know where wisdom is found.

According to the apostle Paul, true wisdom is found in Jesus Christ. When Paul wrote the letter we call 1 Corinthians, he wrote it for a group of Christians who were trying to mix Christian wisdom and pagan philosophy, the "wisdom of God" and the "wisdom of this world." Paul showed them how foolish they were in this attempt.

Paul explains in this letter what true wisdom is, how to get it, and how to use it to the glory of God and the building up of His church. If we want to "be wise," there is a price to pay, *but the price to pay for being foolish is even greater!*

First Corinthians is a letter about real people with real problems, a letter that magnifies Jesus Christ, the cross, and the wisdom of God in Christ. It is a letter we all need to study today.

So, don't just get smart. Be wise.

Follow the way of love and eagerly desire spiritual gifts.

1 CORINTHIANS 14:1

Day 1

Problems in the Church

Read 1 Corinthians 1:1–3

> *To the church of God in Corinth, to those sanctified in*
> *Christ Jesus and called to be holy, together with all those everywhere*
> *who call on the name of our Lord Jesus Christ.*
>
> 1 CORINTHIANS 1:2

Jesus, yes! The church, no!" Remember when that slogan was popular among young people in the sixties? They certainly could have used it with sincerity in Corinth back in AD 56, because the local church there was in serious trouble. Sad to say, the problems did not stay within the church family; they were known by the unbelievers outside the church.

To begin with, the church at Corinth was a *defiled* church. Some of its members were guilty of sexual immorality; others got drunk; still others were using the grace of God to excuse worldly living. It was also a *divided* church, with at least four different groups competing for leadership (v. 12). This meant it was a *disgraced* church. Instead of glorifying God, it was hindering the progress of the gospel.

How did this happen? The members of the church permitted the sins of the city to get into the local assembly. Corinth was a polluted city, filled with every kind of vice and worldly pleasure. It was also a proud, philosophical city, with many itinerant teachers promoting their speculations.

Any time there are proud people, depending on human wisdom, adopting the lifestyle of the world, there are going to be problems.

⁂

Applying God's Truth:

1. In what ways is your church like the church at Corinth? How is it different?

2. How is your church influenced by the problems of the city where it is located?

3. What, personally, do you hope to accomplish by reading through the book of 1 Corinthians?

Day 2

Divided Loyalties

Read 1 Corinthians 1:4–17

I appeal to you, brothers, in the name of our Lord Jesus Christ,
that all of you agree with one another so that there may be
no divisions among you and that you may be perfectly
united in mind and thought.

1 CORINTHIANS 1:10

A Christian photographer friend told me about a lovely wedding that he "covered." The bride and groom came out of the church, heading for the limousine, when the bride suddenly left her husband and ran to a car parked across the street! The motor was running, and a man was at the wheel; off they drove, leaving the bridegroom speechless. The driver of the "getaway car" turned out to be an old boyfriend of the bride, a man who had boasted that "he could get her any time he wanted her." Needless to say, the husband had the marriage annulled.

When a man and woman pledge their love to one other, they are set apart for each other; and any other relationship outside of marriage is sinful. Just so, Christians belong completely to Jesus Christ; they are set apart for Him and Him alone. But they are also part of a worldwide fellowship, the church, "all those everywhere who call on the name of our Lord Jesus Christ" (v. 2). Defiled and unfaithful believers not only sin against the Lord, but also sin against their fellow Christians.

Applying God's Truth:

1. Can you identify any ways your church has deserted Jesus to pursue worldly interests?

2. On a personal level, are there any activities you need to give up in order to follow Jesus more completely?

3. How can the sin of one person affect the church as a whole?

Day 3

Low and Mighty

Read 1 Corinthians 1:18–31

> *God chose the foolish things of the world to shame the wise; God chose*
> *the weak things of the world to shame the strong.*
>
> 1 CORINTHIANS 1:27

God chose the foolish, the weak, the lowly, and the despised to show the proud world its need and His grace. The lost world admires birth, social status, financial success, power, and recognition. But none of these things can guarantee eternal life.

The message and miracle of God's grace in Jesus Christ utterly put to shame the high and mighty people of this world. The wise of this world cannot understand how God changes sinners into saints, and the mighty of this world are helpless to duplicate the miracle. God's "foolishness" confounds the wise; God's "weakness" confounds the mighty!

The annals of church history are filled with the accounts of great sinners whose lives were transformed by the power of the gospel. In my own ministry, as in the ministry of most pastors and preachers, I have seen amazing things take place that the lawyers and psychologists could not understand. We have seen delinquent teenagers become successful students and useful citizens. We have seen marriages restored and homes reclaimed, much to the amazement of the courts.

And why does God reveal the foolishness and the weakness of this present world system, even with its philosophy and religion? "So that no one may boast before him" (v. 29). Salvation must be wholly of grace; otherwise, God cannot get the glory.

Applying God's Truth:

1. Can you think of a recent lesson you have learned from someone most people would consider foolish, weak, or lowly?

2. What is an amazing act of God you have witnessed lately that "confounds" those who are wise and/or powerful?

3. Are you content with being perceived by others as foolish and weak? Explain.

Day 4

Mixed Messages

Read 1 Corinthians 2:1–5

> *I resolved to know nothing while I was with you except*
> *Jesus Christ and him crucified.*
>
> 1 CORINTHIANS 2:2

My wife was at the wheel of our car as we drove to Chicago, and I was in the copilot's seat reading the page proofs of another author's book that a publisher had asked me to review. Occasionally I would utter a grunt and then a groan, and finally I shook my head and said, "Oh no! I can't believe it!"

"I take it you don't like the book," she said. "Something wrong with it?"

"You bet there is!" I replied. "Just about everything is wrong with it, because this man does not know what the message of the gospel really is!"

There was a time, however, when that author had been faithful to the gospel. But over the years, he had begun to take a philosophical (and, I fear, political) approach to the gospel. The result was a hybrid message that was no gospel at all.

It is worth noting that when Paul ministered in Corinth, he obeyed our Lord's commission and preached the gospel (Mark 16:15 KJV). What had happened at Corinth after Paul's departure is happening in churches today: People are mixing philosophy (human wisdom) with the gospel (God's revealed message), and this mixture is causing confusion and division. Different preachers have their own "approach" to God's message, and some even invent their own vocabulary! Paul urged his readers to return to the fundamentals of the gospel message.

Applying God's Truth:

1. In what ways do some people try to combine ungodly philosophies with the truth of the gospel?

2. In what ways do some people try to combine a political agenda with the truth of the gospel?

3. How can you stay focused on "Jesus Christ and him crucified" without getting bogged down in philosophy and politics?

Day 5

Salvation: A United Effort

Read 1 Corinthians 2:6–10

"No eye has seen, no ear has heard, no mind has conceived what God has prepared for those who love him"—but God has revealed it to us by his Spirit.

1 CORINTHIANS 2:9–10

Salvation involves all three persons in the Godhead. No one can be saved apart from the Father's electing grace, the Son's loving sacrifice, and the Spirit's ministry of conviction and regeneration. It is not enough to say, "I believe in God." What God? Unless it is "the God and Father of our Lord Jesus Christ" (Eph. 1:3), there can be no salvation.

This Trinitarian aspect of salvation helps us to understand better some of the mysteries of our own salvation. Many people get confused (or frightened) when they hear about election and predestination, so let me illustrate these terms from my own experience. As far as God the Father is concerned, I was saved when He chose me in Christ before the foundation of the world (Eph. 1:4 KJV), but I knew nothing about that the night I was saved! It was a hidden part of God's wonderful eternal plan.

As far as God the Son is concerned, I was saved when He died for me on the cross. He died for the sins of the whole world, yet the whole world is not saved. This is where the Spirit comes in: As far as the Spirit is concerned, I was saved on May 12, 1945, at a Youth for Christ rally where I heard Billy Graham (then a young evangelist) preach the gospel. It was then that the Holy Spirit applied the Word to my heart, I believed, and God saved me.

Applying God's Truth:

1. In what ways did you observe the activity of each member of the Godhead in regard to your salvation?

2. What would you consider a "hidden part of God's wonderful eternal plan" for your own life?

3. Why do you think God allows salvation to be such a "mystery" to us?

Day 6

Speaking the Language

Read 1 Corinthians 2:11–16

This is what we speak, not in words taught us by human wisdom but in words taught by the Spirit, expressing spiritual truths in spiritual words.

1 Corinthians 2:13

Each of our four children has a different vocation. We have a pastor, a nurse, an electronics designer, and a secretary in a commercial real estate firm. Each of the children had to learn a specialized vocabulary in order to succeed. The only one I really understand is the pastor.

Successful Christians learn the vocabulary of the Spirit and make use of it. They know the meaning of justification, sanctification, adoption, propitiation, election, inspiration, and so forth. In understanding God's vocabulary, they come to understand God's Word and God's will for their lives. If engineering students can grasp the technical terms of chemistry, physics, or electronics, why should it be difficult for Christians, taught by the Spirit, to grasp the vocabulary of Christian truth?

Yet I hear church members say, "Don't preach doctrine. Just give us heartwarming sermons that will encourage us!" Sermons based on what? If they are not based on doctrine, they will accomplish nothing! "But doctrine is so dull!" people complain. Not if it is presented the way the Bible presents it. Doctrine is exciting! What a thrill to be able to study the Bible and let the Spirit teach us "the deep things of God" (v. 10).

Applying God's Truth:

1. How would you define the Christian concept of justification? Sanctification? Adoption? Propitiation? Election? Inspiration?

2. If your understanding of Christian doctrine isn't what you want it to be, what are some better options to learn what you want to know?

3. As you learn "the vocabulary of the Spirit," do you foresee any potential problems with *using* Christian "lingo"? Explain.

Day 7

Watch Your Diet

Read 1 Corinthians 3:1–9

> *I gave you milk, not solid food, for you were not yet ready for it.*
> *Indeed, you are still not ready. You are still worldly.*

1 CORINTHIANS 3:2–3

What are the marks of maturity? For one thing, we can tell mature people by *their diet*. As I write this chapter, we are watching our grandson and our granddaughter grow up. Becky is still being nursed by her mother, but Jonathan now sits at the table and uses his little cup and (with varying degrees of success) his tableware. As children grow, they learn to eat different food. They graduate from milk to meat.

What is the difference? The usual answer is that "milk" represents the easy things in the Word, while "solid food" (or "meat") represents the hard doctrines. But I disagree with that traditional explanation, and my proof is Hebrews 5:11–14. That passage seems to teach that "milk" represents what Jesus Christ did on earth, while "solid food" concerns what He is doing now in heaven. The writer of Hebrews wanted to teach his readers about the present heavenly priesthood of Jesus Christ, but his readers were so immature, he could not do it.

It is not difficult to determine believers' spiritual maturity, or immaturity, if we discover what kind of "diet" they enjoy. Immature believers know little about the present ministry of Christ in heaven. They know the *facts* about our Lord's life and ministry on earth, but not the *truths* about His present ministry in heaven. They live on

"Bible stories" and not Bible doctrines. They have no understanding of 1 Corinthians 2:6–7.

Applying God's Truth:

1. What food(s) would you say best represent(s) your current spiritual "diet"? Why?

2. If "milk" represents what Jesus did on earth and "meat" represents what He is doing now in heaven, which "food group" are you more familiar with? How can you get a better "balanced diet"?

3. Can you give a personal example about someone who knows spiritual "facts," but not necessarily spiritual "truths"?

Day 8

Secrets of Church Success

Read 1 Corinthians 3:10–23

Do not deceive yourselves. If any one of you thinks he is wise by the standards of this age, he should become a "fool" so that he may become wise.

1 CORINTHIANS 3:18

Young ministers often asked Dr. G. Campbell Morgan the secret of his pulpit success. Morgan replied, "I always say to them the same thing—work; hard work; and again, work!" Morgan was in his study at six o'clock each morning, digging treasures out of the Bible. We can find wood, hay, and straw (v. 12) in our backyard, and it will not take too much effort to pick them up. But if we want gold, silver, and jewels, *we have to dig for them.* Lazy preachers and Sunday school teachers will have much to answer for at the judgment seat of Christ—and so will preachers and teachers who *steal* material from others instead of studying and making it their own.

It comes as a shock to some church members that we cannot manage a local church the same way we run a business. This does not mean we should not follow good business principles, but the operation is totally different. There is a wisdom of this world that works for the world, but it will not work for the church.

The world depends on promotion, prestige, and the influence of money and important people. The church depends on prayer, the power of the Spirit, humility, sacrifice, and service. The church that imitates the world may seem to succeed in time, but it will turn to ashes in eternity.

Applying God's Truth:

1. What would you say best describes the type of "building" you have been doing on the spiritual foundation that Jesus has laid: straw, hay, wood, precious stones, silver, or gold? Explain.

2. What successful business principles do you think will work for the church? Which ones will not?

3. In what ways do you try to help your church be the best it can be?

Day 9

No Place for Pride

Read 1 Corinthians 4:1–13

> *It seems to me that God has put us apostles on display at the end of*
> *the procession, like men condemned to die in the arena. We have been*
> *made a spectacle to the whole universe, to angels as well as to men.*

1 CORINTHIANS 4:9

There is no place for pride in the ministry. If a truly great leader like Paul considered himself "on display at the end of the procession," where does this leave the rest of us? Church members are wrong when they measure ministers by standards other than those God has given. They are also wrong when they boast about their favorite preachers. This is not to say that faithful servants should not be recognized and honored (1 Thess. 5:12–13), but in all things, God must be glorified.

Paul was a fool according to the standards of the world. Had he remained a Jewish rabbi, he could have attained great heights in the Jewish religion (Gal. 1:14). Or had he sided with the Jewish legalists in the Jerusalem church and not ministered to the Gentiles, he could have avoided a great deal of persecution (Acts 15; 21:17ff).

The Corinthians were wise in their own eyes, but they were actually fools in the sight of God. By depending on the wisdom and the standards of the world, they were acting like fools. Many times to be spiritually wise is to become foolish in the eyes of the world (1 Cor. 3:18). I often find myself quoting those words of martyred Jim Elliot: "He is no fool who gives what he cannot keep to gain what he cannot lose."

Applying God's Truth:

1. What specific ways can you think of that pride has damaged the church as a whole? How about your local church?

2. Do you think congregation members help contribute to the pride of some preachers? How can this potential problem be kept to a minimum?

3. What are some things you "cannot keep"? What are the things you "cannot lose"?

Day 10

Discipline Versus Disobedience

Read 1 Corinthians 4:14–21

The kingdom of God is not a matter of talk but of power.
1 CORINTHIANS 4:20

A child's will must be broken, but not destroyed. Until a colt is broken, it is dangerous and useless, but once it learns to obey, it becomes gentle and useful. Pride is a terrible thing in the Christian life and in the church. The yeast of sin (5:6–8) had made the Corinthians "puffed up," even to the point of saying in essence, "Paul will not come to us! His bark is worse than his bite!" (2 Cor. 10:8–11).

In the past Paul had been patient with their disobedience, but in this letter he warned them that the time had come for discipline. Paul was not like the tolerant modern mother who shouted at her spoiled son, "This is the last time I'm going to tell you for the last time!"

Faithful parents must discipline their children. It is not enough to teach them and be an example before them; parents must also punish them when they rebel and refuse to obey. Paul would have preferred to come to the Corinthians with meekness and deal with their sins in a gentle manner, but their own attitude made this approach difficult. They were puffed up—and even proud of their disobedience (1 Cor. 5:1–2)!

The contrast in this paragraph is between *speech* and *power*, words and deeds. The arrogant Corinthians had no problem "talking big," the way children often will do, but they could not back up their talk with their "walk." Their religion was only in words. Paul was prepared to back up his "talk" with power, with deeds that would reveal their sins and God's holiness.

Applying God's Truth:

1. At what point did you move from needing to be disciplined by others into taking responsibility for self-discipline?

2. How does a lack of self-discipline among its members cause problems in *today's* church?

3. In what specific area(s) is it hardest to discipline yourself? How can you persevere even though it is difficult?

Day 11

Shape Up or Ship Out

Read 1 Corinthians 5

*It is actually reported that there is sexual immorality among you,
and of a kind that does not occur even among pagans:
A man has his father's wife. And you are proud!*

1 CORINTHIANS 5:1–2

The people at Corinth were puffed up. They were boasting of the
fact that their church was so "open minded" that even fornicators
could be members in good standing! The sin in question was a form
of incest: A professed Christian (and a member of the church) was living with his stepmother in a permanent alliance. Since Paul did not
pass judgment on the woman (vv. 9–13), we assume that she was not
a member of the assembly and probably not even a Christian. This
kind of sin was condemned by the Old Testament law as well as by the
laws of the Gentile nations. Paul shamed the church by saying, "Even
the unsaved Gentiles don't practice this kind of sin!"

While Christians are not to judge one another's motives or ministries, we are certainly expected to be honest about each other's
conduct. In my own pastoral ministry, I have never enjoyed having to
initiate church discipline, but since it is commanded in the Scriptures,
we must obey God and set personal feelings aside.

Paul prescribed here an official church meeting at which the
offender should be dealt with according to divine instructions. Public
sin must be publicly judged and condemned. The sin was not to be
"swept under the rug"; for, after all, it was known far and wide even
among the unsaved outside the church.

Applying God's Truth:

1. If you had been a member of the assembly at Corinth, how do you think you would have been affected by the blatant sin within the church?

2. What issues in today's church might attract similar attention from the secular world?

3. Do you have guidelines to help determine whether to (1) dismiss a problem as a "weaker brother" issue, (2) forgive the sin and ignore it, or (3) see it as a danger and confront the person? If not, do you *need* such guidelines?

Day 12

Loss Suits

Read 1 Corinthians 6:1–8

> *The very fact that you have lawsuits among you means you*
> *have been completely defeated already. Why not rather*
> *be wronged? Why not rather be cheated?*
>
> 1 CORINTHIANS 6:7

The church at Corinth was rapidly losing its testimony in the city. Not only did the unsaved know about the immorality in the assembly, but they were also aware of the lawsuits involving members of the church. Not only were there sins of the flesh, but also sins of the spirit.

Paul detected three tragedies in this situation. First, *the believers were presenting a poor testimony to the lost.* Even the unbelieving Jews dealt with their civil cases in their own synagogue courts. To take the problems of Christians and discuss them before the "unjust" (v. 1 KJV) and "unbelievers" (v. 6) was to weaken the testimony of the gospel.

Second, *the congregation had failed to live up to its full position in Christ.* Since the saints will one day participate in the judgment of the world and even of fallen angels (vv. 2–3), they ought to be able to settle their differences here on earth. The Corinthians boasted of their great spiritual gifts. Why, then, did they not use them in solving their problems?

There was a third tragedy: *The members suing each other had already lost* (v. 7). Even if some of them won their cases, they had incurred a far greater loss in their disobedience to the Word of God.

Better to lose money or possessions than to lose a brother and lose their testimony as well.

Applying God's Truth:

1. Do you think Paul's plea for Christians to avoid lawsuits between each other still applies? Why?

2. On a scale of 1 (least) to 10 (most), how much anger do you feel when someone takes advantage of you? How could the number eventually be lower?

3. Rather than secular lawsuits, what are some other options Christians today could pursue when they feel wronged by a fellow believer?

Day 13

The Best Sex

Read 1 Corinthians 6:9–20

*Flee from sexual immorality. All other sins a man commits are
outside his body, but he who sins sexually sins against his own body.*

1 CORINTHIANS 6:18

There is certainly excitement and enjoyment in sexual experience
outside of marriage, *but there is not enrichment.* Having sex outside of marriage is like a man robbing a bank: He gets something, but
it is not his and he will one day pay for it. Sex within marriage can be
like a man putting money into a bank: There are safety and security,
and he will collect dividends.

Paul referred to the creation account to explain the seriousness of
sexual sin (vv. 16–17). When a man and woman join their bodies, *the
entire personality is involved.* There is a much deeper experience, a
"oneness" that brings with it deep and lasting consequences. Paul
warned that sexual sin is the most serious sin a man can commit
against his body, for it involves the whole person (v. 18).

Paul did not suggest that being joined to a harlot was the equiva-
lent of marriage, for marriage also involves *commitment.* When two
people pledge their love and faithfulness to each other, they lay a
strong foundation on which to build. Marriage protects sex and
enables the couple, committed to each other, to grow in this wonderful experience.

In my pastoral counseling, I have had to help married couples
whose relationship was falling apart because of the consequences of

premarital sex, as well as extramarital sex. The harvest of sowing to the flesh is sometimes delayed, but it is certain (Gal. 6:7–8). How sad it is to live with the consequences of *forgiven* sin.

Applying God's Truth:

1. In what ways is sex *enriched* through marriage? Explain.

2. How is premarital or extramarital sex a sin "against [one's] own body"?

3. Can you think of some specific situations where sexual sin was forgiven, yet the person(s) involved still had to "live with the consequences"?

Day 14

A Better Yield

Read 1 Corinthians 7:1–24

The wife's body does not belong to her alone but also to her husband. In the same way, the husband's body does not belong to him alone but also to his wife.

1 CORINTHIANS 7:4

As in all things, the spiritual must govern the physical, for the bodies of believers are God's temples (6:19). The husband and wife may abstain from sex in order to devote their full interest to prayer and fasting (7:5), but they must not use this abstinence as an excuse for prolonged separation. Paul encouraged Christian partners to be "in tune" with each other in matters both spiritual and physical.

Not only did the Corinthian church ask Paul about celibacy (vv. 1–9), but they also asked him about divorce (vv. 10–16). He wrote that if divorce does occur, the parties should remain unmarried or seek reconciliation. It has been my experience as a pastor that when a husband and wife are yielded to the Lord and when they seek to please each other in the marriage relationship, the marriage will be so satisfying that neither partner will think of looking elsewhere for fulfillment.

"There are no sex problems in marriage," a Christian counselor once told me, "only personality problems with sex as one of the symptoms." The present frightening trend of increased divorces among Christians (and even among the clergy) must break the heart of God.

Applying God's Truth:

1. For what reasons do you think married couples begin to withhold sex from each other? What are the potential consequences of doing so?

2. What signs do you detect in today's society that suggest husbands and wives aren't yielding to each other (and God) as they should?

3. What advice would you offer a Christian couple on the brink of divorce?

Day 15

Making Marriage Last

Read 1 Corinthians 7:25–40

A woman is bound to her husband as long as he lives. But if her husband dies, she is free to marry anyone she wishes, but he must belong to the Lord.

1 CORINTHIANS 7:39

It is God's will that the marriage union be permanent, a lifetime commitment. There is no place in Christian marriage for a "trial marriage," nor is there any room for the "escape-hatch" attitude: "If the marriage doesn't work, we can always get a divorce."

For this reason, marriage must be built on something sturdier than good looks, money, romantic excitement, and social acceptance. There must be Christian commitment, character, and maturity. There must be a willingness to grow, to learn from each other, to forgive and forget, to minister to one another.

Paul closed the section by telling the widows that they were free to marry, but the man they marry "must belong to the Lord" (v. 39). This means that they must not only marry believers, but marry in the will of God. Paul's counsel was that they remain single, but he left the decision to them.

God has put "walls" around marriage, not to make it a prison, but to make it a safe fortress. The person who considers marriage a prison should not get married. When two people are lovingly and joyfully committed to each other—and to their Lord—the experience of marriage is one of enrichment and fulfillment. The partners grow together and discover the richness of serving the Lord as a "team" in their home and church.

Applying God's Truth:

1. Based on personal observations, what would you say are the most common reasons for divorce?

2. Now, thinking of the couples you know who have been together for a long time, what do you see as the "secrets" of a strong marriage?

3. In what ways do you feel people today take marriage (and remarriage) too lightly?

Day 16

Puffy "I"s and "Know"s

Read 1 Corinthians 8

We know that we all possess knowledge. Knowledge puffs up, but love builds up.
1 CORINTHIANS 8:1

Love and knowledge must go together. It has well been said, "Knowledge without love is brutality, but love without knowledge is hypocrisy." Paul's great concern was that the strong saints help the weaker saints to grow and to stop being weak saints. Some people have the false notion that the *strong* Christians are the ones who live by rules and regulations and who get offended when others exercise their freedom in Christ, but such is not the case. It is the *weak* Christians who must have the security of law and who are afraid to use their freedom in Christ. It is the weak Christians who are prone to judge and criticize stronger believers and to stumble over what they do. This, of course, makes it difficult for the stronger saints to minister to their weaker brothers and sisters.

It is here that love enters the picture, for "love builds up" and puts others first. When spiritual knowledge is used in love, stronger Christians can take the hand of weaker Christians and help them to stand and walk so as to enjoy their freedom in Christ. *It is impossible to force-feed immature believers and transform them into giants.* Knowledge must be mixed with love; otherwise, the saints will end up with "big heads" instead of enlarged hearts.

Applying God's Truth:

1. Do you know anyone who has "knowledge without love"? How about "love without knowledge"? How do you relate to such people?

2. How has someone used a combination of love and knowledge to make you a stronger Christian?

3. How are *you* using love and knowledge to help weaker Christians? Can you think of anyone who could use some help?

Day 17

Not in It for the Money

Read 1 Corinthians 9:1–18

What then is my reward? Just this: that in preaching the gospel I may offer it free of charge, and so not make use of my rights in preaching it.

1 CORINTHIANS 9:18

It is unfortunate when the ministry of the gospel is sometimes hindered by an overemphasis on money. The unsaved world is convinced that most preachers and missionaries are only involved in "religious rackets" to take money from innocent people. No doubt there are "religious racketeers" in the world today, people who "use" religion to exploit others and control them. We would certainly not agree with their purposes or their practices. We must make sure that nothing we do in our own ministry gives the impression that we are of their number.

A wrong attitude toward money has hindered the gospel from the earliest days of the church. Simon the magician thought he could buy the gift of the Holy Spirit with money (Acts 8:18–24). Ananias and Sapphira loved money more than they loved the truth, and God killed them (5:1–10).

For eighteen fruitful years, Dr. H. A. Ironside served as pastor of Moody Church in Chicago. I recall the first time I heard him announce an offering. He said, "We ask God's people to give generously. If you are not a believer in Jesus Christ, we do not ask you to give. We have a gift for you—eternal life through faith in Christ!" He made it clear that the offering was for believers, lest the unsaved in the congregation stumble over money and then reject the gospel.

Applying God's Truth:

1. What are some misperceptions about the church formed by people who witness "religious racketeers"?

2. Do you think money should ever be discussed publicly at church? To what extent?

3. How can money propel the cause of the gospel? How can it become a hindrance?

Day 18

Run for Your (Spiritual) Life

Read 1 Corinthians 9:19–27

*Run in such a way as to get the prize. Everyone who competes
in the games goes into strict training. They do it to get a crown that
will not last; but we do it to get a crown that will last forever.*

1 CORINTHIANS 9:24–25

Athletes must be disciplined if they are to win the prize. Discipline means giving up the good and the better for the best. Athletes must watch their diet as well as their hours. They must smile and say, "No, thank you," when people offer them fattening desserts or invite them to late-night parties. There is nothing wrong with food or fun, but if they interfere with people's highest goals, then they are hindrances and not helps.

We Christians do not run the race in order to get to heaven. We are in the race because we have been saved through faith in Jesus Christ. Only Greek citizens were allowed to participate in the games, and they had to obey the rules both in their training and in their performing; any contestant found breaking the training rules was automatically disqualified. The famous Native American athlete, Jim Thorpe, had to return his Olympic gold medals because it was discovered that he had previously played on a professional team.

In order to give up his rights and have the joy of winning lost souls, Paul had to discipline himself. That is the emphasis of 1 Corinthians 9: Authority (rights) must be balanced by discipline. If we want to serve the Lord and win His reward and approval, we must pay the price.

Applying God's Truth:

1. In what ways has your spiritual life been like a race so far?

2. What do you expect to "win" when you get to the "finish line"?

3. Though "discipline" is often used in a negative context, how is it a positive attribute in physical sports and spiritual development?

Day 19

Inconsistently Consistent

Read 1 Corinthians 10

> *"Everything is permissible"—but not everything is beneficial.*
> *"Everything is permissible"—but not everything is constructive.*
> *Nobody should seek his own good, but the good of others.*
>
> 1 CORINTHIANS 10:23–24

Paul probably appeared inconsistent to those who did not understand his principles of Christian living. At times, he would eat what the Gentiles were eating. At other times, he would eat only "kosher" food with the Jews. But instead of being inconsistent, he was actually living *consistently* by the principles he laid down in these chapters of 1 Corinthians.

A weather vane seems inconsistent, first pointing in one direction and then in another. But a weather vane is always consistent: It always points in the direction in which the wind is blowing. That is what makes it useful.

As Christians we *do* have freedom. This freedom was purchased for us by Jesus Christ, so it is very precious. Freedom comes from knowledge: "You will know the truth, and the truth will set you free" (John 8:32). However, knowledge must be balanced by love; otherwise, it will tear down instead of build up.

The way we use our freedom and relate to others indicates whether we are mature in Christ. Strong and weak Christians need to work together in love to edify one another and glorify Jesus.

Applying God's Truth:

1. Can you think of ways that obedience to God's commands may have made you appear inconsistent to other people from time to time?

2. Do you find it more comfortable to have hard and fast rules for behavior or the freedom to be somewhat inconsistent? Explain.

3. In what ways can we misuse Christian freedom if we aren't careful?

Day 20

Order in the Church

Read 1 Corinthians 11:1–16

> *I want you to realize that the head of every man is Christ,*
> *and the head of the woman is man, and the head of Christ is God.*
> 1 CORINTHIANS 11:3

Eastern society at this time was very jealous over its women. Except for the temple prostitutes, the women wore long hair and, in public, wore a covering over their heads. (Paul did not use the word "veil," i.e., a covering over the face. In church, the woman put her regular shawl over her head, and this covering symbolized her submission and purity.) For the Christian women to appear in public without the covering, let alone to pray and share the Word in church, was both daring and blasphemous.

Paul sought to restore order by reminding the Corinthians that God had made a difference between men and women, that each had a proper place in God's economy. There were also appropriate customs that symbolized these relationships and reminded both men and women of their correct places in the divine scheme. Paul did not say, or even hint, that *difference* meant *inequality* or *inferiority*. If there is to be peace in the church, then there must be some kind of order; and order of necessity involves rank. However, *rank* and *quality* are two different things. The captain has a higher rank than the private, but the private may be a better person.

Applying God's Truth:

1. What are some of the expectations for the men and women in your church that help ensure order?

2. Considering that the worship service is only an hour or so out of a week, do you think it is wrong to submit your personal feelings to achieve order? Explain.

3. If someone feels inferior or unequal at church, what are that individual's options?

Day 21

Whose Supper Is This, Anyway?

Read 1 Corinthians 11:17–34

> *A man ought to examine himself before he eats*
> *of the bread and drinks of the cup.*
>
> 1 CORINTHIANS 11:28

From the beginning of the church, it was customary for the believers to eat together. It was an opportunity for fellowship and for sharing with those who were less privileged. No doubt the church climaxed this meal by observing the Lord's Supper.

The *"agape* feast" (from the Greek word for "love") was part of the worship at Corinth, but some serious abuses had crept in. For one thing, there were various cliques in the church, and people ate with their own "crowd" instead of fellowshipping with the whole church family (v. 18).

Another fault was selfishness: The rich people brought a great deal of food for themselves, while the poorer members went hungry. And some of the members were even getting drunk (vv. 20–21).

Of course, the divisions at the dinner were but evidence of the deeper problems in the church. The Corinthians thought they were advanced believers, when in reality they were but little children. Paul did not suggest that they abandon the feast, but rather that they restore its proper meaning. The *"agape* feast" should have been an opportunity for edification, but they were using it as a time for embarrassment.

Applying God's Truth:

1. Do you recognize any of these early church problems (or similar ones) in your own church "fellowships"?

2. What would you suggest to make your church meetings more edifying for all people involved?

3. How could your "regular" meetings bring more glory to God?

Day 22

Body Building

Read 1 Corinthians 12

If one part [of the body] suffers, every part suffers with it;
if one part is honored, every part rejoices with it.

1 CORINTHIANS 12:26

Diversity in the body is an evidence of the wisdom of God. Each member needs the other members, and no member can afford to become independent. When a part of the human body becomes independent, there is a serious problem that could lead to sickness and even death. In a healthy human body, the various members cooperate with one other and even compensate for each other when a crisis occurs. The instant any part of the body says to any other part, "I don't need you!" it begins to weaken and die and create problems for the whole body.

A famous preacher was speaking at a ministers' meeting, and he took time before and after the meeting to shake hands with the pastors and chat with them. A friend asked him, "Why take time for a group of men you may never see again?" The world-renowned preacher smiled and said, "Well, I may be where I am because of them! Anyway, if I didn't need them on the way up, I may need them on the way down!" No Christian servant can say to any other servant, "My ministry can get along without you!"

❦

Applying God's Truth:

1. In terms of a human body, what "part" would you say you are in the church? Why?

2. What is a recent situation in which you suffered because someone else did? When have you rejoiced because someone else was joyful?

3. Who are some people you have been trying to "get along without" whom you may need to start working *with* instead?

Day 23

Not Enough Love?

Read 1 Corinthians 13

> *If I give all I possess to the poor and surrender my body*
> *to the flames, but have not love, I gain nothing.*
>
> 1 CORINTHIANS 13:3

It was Jonathan Swift, the satirical author of *Gulliver's Travels*, who said, "We have just enough religion to make us hate, but not enough to make us love one another." Spiritual gifts, no matter how exciting and wonderful, are useless and even destructive if they are not ministered in love. In all three of the "body" passages in Paul's letters, there is an emphasis on love. The main evidence of maturity in the Christian life is a growing love for God and for God's people, as well as a love for lost souls. It has well been said that love is the "circulatory system" of the body of Christ.

Few chapters in the Bible have suffered more misinterpretation and misapplication than 1 Corinthians 13. Divorced from its context, it becomes "a hymn to love" or a sentimental sermon on Christian brotherhood. Many people fail to see that Paul was still dealing with the Corinthians' problems when he wrote these words: the abuse of the gift of tongues, division in the church, envy of others' gifts, selfishness (remember the lawsuits?), impatience with one another in the public meetings, and behavior that was disgracing the Lord.

The only way spiritual gifts can be used creatively is when Christians are motivated by love.

Applying God's Truth:

1. Can you think of people who try to use spiritual gifts without being loving as well? What do you think of their ministries?

2. Do you think love is sweet and natural or difficult and rare? Explain.

3. Of all of your current relationships and situations, where would you say love is *most* needed?

Day 24

Do You Understand?

Read 1 Corinthians 14:1–25

> *Follow the way of love and eagerly desire spiritual gifts.*
> 1 CORINTHIANS 14:1

A ministry that does not build up will tear down, no matter how "spiritual" it may seem. When we explain and apply the Word of God to individual lives, we have a ministry of edification. In this section, Paul repeatedly shows concern for *understanding*. It is not enough for the minister to impart information to people; the people must receive it if it is to do them any good. The seed that is received in the good ground is the seed that bears fruit, but this means that there must be an *understanding* of the Word of God (Matt. 13:23). If believers want to be edified, they must prepare their hearts to receive the Word (1 Thess. 2:13). Not everybody who listens really hears (Matt. 13:13–15).

The famous Congregationalist minister Dr. Joseph Parker preached at an important meeting and afterward was approached by a man who criticized a minor point in the sermon. Parker listened patiently to the man's criticism and then asked, "And what *else* did you get from the message?" This remark simply withered the critic, who then disappeared into the crowd. Too often we are quick to judge the sermon instead of allowing the Word of God to judge us.

Applying God's Truth:

1. In what ways have people "built you up" this week? What opportunities did they miss?

2. When have you recently been guilty of listening without hearing?

3. What are three things you can do to be a more understanding person from now on? Specifically, how can you better understand people who don't agree with you on the issue of speaking in tongues?

Day 25

Group Consideration

Read 1 Corinthians 14:26–35

> *God is not a God of disorder but of peace.*
> 1 Corinthians 14:33

We must use the Word of God to test every message we hear, asking the Spirit to guide us. There are false teachers in the world, and we must beware (1 John 4:1). But even true teachers and preachers do not know everything and sometimes make mistakes. Each of us must evaluate the message and apply it to his or her own heart (Acts 17:11).

Our public meetings are more formal than those of the early church, so it is not likely that we need to worry about the order of the service. But in our more informal meetings, we need to consider one another and maintain order. I recall being in a testimony meeting where a woman took forty minutes telling a boring experience and, as a result, destroyed the spirit of the meeting.

Evangelist D. L. Moody was leading a service and asked a man to pray. Taking advantage of his opportunity, the man prayed on and on. Sensing that the prayer was killing the meeting instead of blessing it, Moody spoke up and said, "While our brother finishes his prayer, let us sing a hymn!" Those who are in charge of public meetings need to have discernment—and courage.

Applying God's Truth:

1. If you were a professional church consultant, what objective suggestions would you give your pastor for how to improve your church worship services?

2. Do people at your church tend to abuse the privilege of participating in public worship? Do you think they should be tolerated or confronted? Why?

3. In what ways do you think your church leaders need to have clearer discernment? Additional courage?

Day 26

A Tongues Summary

Read 1 Corinthians 14:36–40

> *Everything should be done in a fitting and orderly way.*
> 1 CORINTHIANS 14:40

It might be helpful to summarize what Paul wrote about the gift of tongues. It was the God-given ability to speak in a known language with which the speaker was not previously acquainted. The purpose was not to win the lost, but to edify the saved. Not every believer had this gift, nor was this gift an evidence of spirituality or the result of a "baptism of the Spirit."

Only three persons were permitted to speak in tongues in one meeting, and they had to do so in order and with interpretation. If there was no interpreter, they had to keep silent. Prophecy was the superior gift, but tongues were not to be despised if they were exercised according to Scripture.

When the foundational work of the apostles and prophets ended, it would seem that the gifts of knowledge, prophecy, and tongues would no longer be needed. "Where there are tongues, they will be stilled" (13:8). Certainly God could give this gift today if He pleased, but I am not prepared to believe that every instance of tongues is divinely energized. Nor would I go so far as to say that all instances of tongues are either satanic or self-induced.

It is unfortunate when believers make tongues a test of fellowship or spirituality. That in itself would alert me that the Spirit may not be at work. Let's keep our priorities straight and major on winning the lost and building the church.

Applying God's Truth:

1. Do you have any questions about the gift of tongues? If so, where can you go to find answers?

2. What do you think 1 Corinthians 13:8 means: "Where there are tongues, they will be stilled"?

3. Why do you think Paul gave so many instructions regarding the proper procedures for speaking in tongues?

Day 27

Paul's Witness

Read 1 Corinthians 15:1–28

> *[Jesus] appeared to James, then to all the apostles, and last of all*
> *he appeared to me also, as to one abnormally born. For I am the least*
> *of the apostles and do not even deserve to be called an apostle.*

1 CORINTHIANS 15:7–9

One of the greatest witnesses of the resurrection was Paul himself, for as an unbeliever he was soundly convinced that Jesus was dead. The radical change in his life—a change that brought him persecution and suffering—is certainly evidence that the Lord had indeed been raised from the dead. Paul made it clear that his salvation was purely an act of God's grace, but that grace worked in and through him as he served the Lord (v. 10).

At this point, Paul's readers would say, "Yes, we agree that *Jesus* was raised from the dead." Then Paul would reply, "If you believe that, then you must believe in the resurrection of *all* the dead!" Christ came as a man, truly human, and experienced all that we experienced, except that He never sinned (Heb. 4:14–15). If there is no resurrection, then Christ was not raised. If He was not raised, there is no gospel to preach. If there is no gospel, then we have believed in vain, and we are still in our sins! If there is no resurrection, then believers who have died have no hope. We will never see them again (1 Cor. 15:12–19)!

The conclusion is obvious: Why be a Christian if we have only suffering in this life and no future glory to anticipate? (In vv. 29–34, Paul expanded this idea.) The resurrection is not just important; it is "of first importance" (vv. 3–4), because all we believe hinges upon it.

Applying God's Truth:

1. Is the resurrection of the dead "of first importance" to you? Give an example.

2. What would you tell a friend who asked, "How do you think you're going to be different after your resurrection?"

3. Can people look at the changes you have made in your life and see God's grace? Why or why not?

Day 28

Victory: Now and Later

Read 1 Corinthians 15:29–58

Thanks be to God! He gives us the victory through our Lord Jesus Christ.
1 CORINTHIANS 15:57

The heavenly kingdom is not made for the kind of bodies we now have, bodies of flesh and blood. So when Jesus returns, the bodies of living believers will instantly be transformed to be like His body (vv. 50–54; 1 John 3:1–3), and the dead believers will be raised with new glorified bodies. Our new bodies will not be subject to decay or death (1 Cor. 15:42–44).

Sigmund Freud, the founder of psychiatry, wrote: "And finally there is the painful riddle of death, for which no remedy at all has yet been found, nor probably ever will be." Christians have victory *in* death and *over* death! Why? Because of the victory of Jesus Christ in His own resurrection. Jesus said: "Because I live, you also will live" (John 14:19).

We share the victory *today*. The literal translation of 1 Corinthians 15:57 is, "But thanks be to God, *who keeps on giving us the victory through our Lord Jesus Christ.*" We experience "the power of his resurrection" (Phil. 3:10). First Corinthians 15:58 is Paul's hymn of praise to the Lord as well as his closing admonition to the church. Because of the assurance of Christ's victory over death, we know that nothing we do for Him will ever be wasted or lost. We can be steadfast in our service, unmovable in suffering, abounding in ministry to others, because we know our labor is not in vain.

Applying God's Truth:

1. What are your fears and concerns about death?

2. In what ways has Jesus provided victory in regard to the things you just listed?

3. In what other areas do you need to experience victory? What steps do you need to take toward more complete victory in your spiritual struggles?

Day 29

Doctrine and Duty

Read 1 Corinthians 16:1–9

> *On the first day of every week, each one of you should set aside*
> *a sum of money in keeping with his income, saving it up, so that*
> *when I come no collections will have to be made.*

1 CORINTHIANS 16:2

It is unfortunate when Christian ministries lose their testimony because they mismanage funds entrusted to them. Every ministry ought to be businesslike in its financial affairs. Paul was very careful not to allow anything to happen that would give his enemies opportunity to accuse him of stealing funds (2 Cor. 8:20–21).

This explains why Paul encouraged the *churches* to share in the offering and to select dependable representatives to help manage it. Paul was not against *individuals* giving personally; in this chapter he named various individuals who assisted him personally (vv. 10–20). This no doubt included helping him with his financial needs. But generally speaking, Christian giving is church centered. Many churches encourage their members to give designated gifts through the church treasury.

It is interesting that Paul mentioned the offering just after his discussion about the resurrection. There were no "chapter breaks" in the original manuscripts, so the readers would go right from Paul's hymn of victory into his discussion about money. Doctrine and duty go together; so do worship and works. Our giving is "not in vain" because our Lord is alive. It is His resurrection power that motivates us to give and to serve.

Applying God's Truth:

1. What connection do you see between Jesus' resurrection and your giving to the church?

2. What procedures does your church have to make sure money is not mismanaged?

3. Do you think monetary giving is all that is required of us, or do you think Paul's guidelines may apply to other kinds of giving as well? Explain.

Day 30

In Conclusion ...

Read 1 Corinthians 16:10–24

Be on your guard; stand firm in the faith; be men
of courage; be strong. Do everything in love.

1 CORINTHIANS 16:13–14

Paul's closing words need not detain us. The "holy kiss" (v. 20) was a common mode of greeting: the men kissing the men and the women kissing the women. If Paul were writing to Western churches today, he would say, "Shake hands with one another."

Paul usually dictated his letters and then took the pen and added his signature. He also added his "benediction of grace" as a mark that the letter was authentic. The word *anathema* (v. 22 KJV) is Aramaic and means "accursed." Not to love Christ means not to believe in Him, and unbelievers are accursed (John 3:16–21). The word *maranatha* is Greek and means "our Lord comes" or (as a prayer) "our Lord, come!" If people love Jesus Christ, they will also "love his appearing" (2 Tim. 4:8 KJV).

Paul had been stern with the Corinthian believers, but he closed his letter by assuring them of his love. After all, "wounds from a friend can be trusted" (Prov. 27:6).

Paul has shared a great deal of spiritual wisdom with us. May we receive it with meekness and put it into practice to the glory of God!

Applying God's Truth:

1. Does your church have a special or unique type of greeting? If not, do you think it could use one?

2. If you had been a first-century Christian reading this epistle for the first time, what questions do you think you might have had for Paul?

3. What three things have you learned (or been reminded of) from 1 Corinthians that you think are most noteworthy?